The Refrigerator Memory

The Refrigerator Memory

Shannon Bramer

Coach House Books

first edition

Published with the assistance of the Canada Council for the Arts
and the Ontario Arts Council. We also acknowledge the support of
the Government of Ontario through the Ontario Book Publishing
Tax Credit Program and the Government of Canada through the
Book Publishing Industry Development Program.

LIBRARY AND ARCHIVES CANADA CATALOGUING IN PUBLICATION

Bramer, Shannon
     The refrigerator memory / Shannon Bramer.

Poems.
ISBN 1-55245-154-2

    I. Title.

PS8553.R269R44 2005   C811'.54   C2005-901258-7

This book is for David Derry
and our sparkly Sadie Glenn

'You know your own difference.'
— Nicholas Gilbert Scott, age four

Contents

Hating Hungry People

The Molested in the Mirror

The Foyer of Formal Feeling

Hating Hungry People

Hating Hungry People

The girl says she is always hungry
but I suspect some other poverty
something cold and sad
in her packed lunch

Yes. Some secret with her silent
egg salad. Some dispute
with the tuna-fish sandwich
cut into terrible triangles. Even this
salted tomato is too large
and unhappy, heart-halved
and runny
                    with seeds

Her chocolate and raisins are no answer
I've always hated hungry people

Will not attend your famished picnic
Will not unfold the checkered blanket

Gerald's Wife Tina

Gerald's wife Tina is driving him crazy, keeps leaving
the table to cry. She's up again curling her hair come midnight:
Fixing Thin Tina All Shadow No Sky.

Tina's got lonely and dying they say: Poor Gerald, Poor Love
in the olden-days way. Go out again, now, go out
for a walk – Gerald feels for his coat and keys in the lock.

Tina had dresses and lipstick in red. Tina's in a ball
now, with the cat
on the bed.

Our Prosthesis

On Saturday night I hid his prosthetic arm. He was drunk, it was easy; when he tried to run after me he stumbled, fell, hit his head on the corner of the coffee table. I was drunk too, sad, acting stupidly. Earlier that night he had been flirting with my sister and I felt neglected and negligible next to her in her pink sweater. I didn't like the way he kept touching her with his false limb; I didn't like the way she kept giggling at the strange feel of the plastic. I had paid for his prosthesis, after all, so perhaps this explains my possessiveness. When we got home we kept drinking. Before bed I started undressing him: his socks, his pants, his underwear, his sweater, his shirt, his arm. He came after me and fell. His forehead bled all over the carpet. I hid his arm in the basement. Dressed his wound. Put him to bed. Showered. Made tea. I read *The Idiot* deep into the night. My sister doesn't even know who Dostoyevsky is.

Love the Clown

It was too bad about Love
who kept his nationality
secret, who never left the house
without his burnt red wig.

They accused him
of being greedy and perverse.
Of touching children
and stealing.

He was a tickler.
And I didn't like being tickled.

Still, it was wrong of the adults
to hurry him, wigless, out of town.
The way we children took to stoning
his car with hard candy.

God in Winter

Instead of church Sarah
goes to tanning salons.
Feeds on light. Stuffs herself
senseless says the Hairstylist.

Butterfly on a Wheel

O, you tug
at his wings,
tear them
away.
From his body:
gentle
child in yellow, see
him strange
as calligraphy, see
your naked
monarch twitch
with grief, black,
no, no
longer himself.

No wings, now
wish the dead
awake, wake
up! Early love
poems
pressed in a book.

O, you tug
at his wings,
tear them
away.

Small Words Inside Sleep

We share a small space, my son and I. That is why I always hear him. Abrupt, broken pieces of word punch themselves out of his tiny mouth as if he had no will; the words will themselves. He sleeps on his back, his hands in two fierce fists. I've asked around but no one seems to know whether or not it is normal for a two-year-old to speak, with such determination, in his sleep.

He is young, the words are ordinary enough, often monosyllabic: *tree, bus, cup, cut, bug, no, sky, rock, tree, bus, cup, cut, bug, no, sky.* I have taken to recording the things I am able to discern. Sometimes he speaks sentences. Once he said: *I need that.* It shocked me to hear him speak so clearly, with such confidence. His small voice in the night sounds a hundred years old.

During the day he speaks so softly I can scarcely hear him. He responds to everyday questions carefully, flushed with embarrassment, as if he knew more about the words than he should. Living with him I have become both fearful and accustomed to a strange, intermittent kind of silence.

What is a young mother to do?

I have told him the plants in our apartment will grow stronger if he talks to them. I'm sure they now know all of his secrets. He is patient and methodical, makes time for all nine of them, turns to the various leaves and flowers and listens in return. Their conversations make me envious. I have tried to hear what the plants have to say, but they remain solemn and tight-lipped with me. This amuses my little son, who quietly laughs at his silly mother kneeling before the fern and spider plants, hair tangled in leaves, trying so hard.

The Photographer

What it means to carry a camera
is to speak out of the empty
frame seeing God, Sky, Road, her return
and faith in the perfection of deserts.
To picture the quiet man's body in the city.
This is what it means to love, to loiter

In forbidden zones, allowing the girl to loiter
there with you, perhaps, taking your camera
away at intervals and sending you into the city
alone. Sometimes we need to come home empty
handed; sick with strange deserts
in mind we will leave and return

With our long memory of the city,
its sights and sounds to repeat and return
to the missing man in the room, his empty
chair. In his cool bed we loiter
in the dark, patient with the camera
and every sense recalling other deserts,

Other times like this when the idea of deserts
confounded us, when we dreamt the city
was made of sand, tugged that camera
down around his neck, no promise of return,
but something of you, hopeful, seemed to loiter
in the mind of the street, the empty

Bed to go back to, your empty
room a perfect void like his deserts,
the window open where you loiter
like a vagrant in your own apartment, the city
loose with lights, the slow lights of return.
You see he is unpacking the camera,

Cradling the camera, testing the empty
        weight of its images, tiny doors of return, her
cold pictures of city, moon, desert.

Lies to Herself

In my thoughts and in my deeds in what I have done and in what I have failed to do. My lies like glass marbles are highly ornamental, they roll and chime, roll

and chime. They whistle, they breathe the sweet breath of muddy flowers despite the swollen down pillows (poor dead goosey) I've used to stifle them.

Sentimental Poem About God

He's wrinkled in his suit.

Santa-like but mean-looking too, drunk
enough to get through a whole black
afternoon.

I see him on the stool
with sparkly dust on his
knees. Scowling and stinking.

His lap looks nice though, somehow
his lap looks nice

and I'd like to crawl
up and be that small
again.

Small as I was
when we first met.

On Buoyancy

The feet and hands all wrong. Toes, elbows, knees fair. The eyes right. The stomach, heart, spleen good. They argue over his brain. Thoughts and ideas, punched down, should pop back up again.

He won't float, they agreed. He'll sink, they said, and sent him back.

Lena and Her Father's Yellow Finches

Lena, you steal grapes from Arabs
Lena, you kiss the darkest boys

She weeps in his red armchair
She sobs on the black and white tile

His finches are yellow, excitable
Yet they die in his house, they die too

Don't touch her cold feathers, Lena
Don't kiss your mother's arms

When her father buys more finches
Lena tends the cage

Lena, you are crying
Lena, let me sweep here

Lena looks for yellow leaves
Under his cold bed

His Peacock Shadow

This is how the story goes:

A peacock became a man
and soon enough fell in love
with a woman.

A female of the highest calibre
with bright black eyes,
muscular arms, hair the colour
of burnt raisin.

The peacock knew pain but
had no memory. At night he felt
the prickly bones of absent feathers
scratching on his skin.

She became his Doctor
and looked like a saint
in her stiff white coat.

He had been referred
to her before, was regal, cocksure
though something
of his diminished strut suggested

a former plumage.

Whenever he got drunk he called
himself a fancy chicken; she
discovered his peacock shadow

after they were married,
while feasting by candlelight.

Bears in the City

Come down from the Velebit mountains
to drink small glasses of white wine

Heavy men with hairy hands   Orphaned bears
sit on stools   Smoking

See the old bear smiles
when he smokes   A dream burns

Out his thoughts   His
smoke climbs inside me

*

I lick my glass I dream his cubs

Purple Turtleneck

See her cherry-red shorts, her yellow
sweater with Martin's spaghetti stain
on the sleeve, the grey scarf her best friend Anna
started knitting and never finished, the needles
still waiting in the forlorn wool
like long pointed teeth

The white underwear mean surrender
and the blue mean swim girl
swim

Sometimes she goes out in her graduation gown
its crumpled green taffeta twisting around her body
so she feels like mint candy

Her pink boots, her neon socks, her Chinese
slippers are all in perfect condition. And when
she wears her father's old jeans, she can't help but feel
the place where his cock has been, consider
the reason she was born.

Home

In the smoke of her cigarette you float up with small
hands and feet   you with long wet hair for Mama to dry

Fernando catching snow-tigers on his tongue
Nona scrubbing potatoes with tree-like hands

In red cathedral cushions he found home
where they burned thin white candles

Dreaming his home where the old tree tips
over apples rotting in the sun, he lay dreaming it

In curling gold wallpaper   loosening her tongue along
the shady edge of his dream

Under two chestnut trees, their strange white blossoms

The Fire-Eater and His Daughter

Once there lived a fire-eater
whose blackened belly bore him
one healthy daughter

And the fire-eater kept her, taught
mouthfuls of fire
and coins from the villagers

But when she grew older
the fire-eater's daughter
drowned her dear father

Down the well he went
like the torch down her throat

O the fire-eater's daughter
put the fire out.

Four Minutes

An ordinary woman, ordinary by International Standards, with nut-brown hair and small nervous eyes, green, and plain because of the short lashes. A nose not large, tiny ears with holes in the lobes but no earrings swinging from them.

All emptiness, this young lady, more because she felt it so than for any other reason. Unmarried. Unlucky. Uncertain, though not so uncertain that she does not pull on her coat late in the evening when she wants to go out. Certain enough that she forgets her scarf, that she drops a glove on the walkway before stepping into the cab.

The driver makes her laugh, freely, because no one else is with them. The driver tells a story about his baby daughter, the same story he told several weeks ago, though he does not remember, does not remember her, this ordinary woman. She would like to pay him to keep driving and keep talking and keep forgetting her because it is nice to be alone with him, because out of the dark sky it is beginning to snow.

When they arrive at the place she has paid him to take her, a small bar, an ordinary bar, a pale pearl strung among a series of bright ones, it is the door that seems less open, the one with snow drifting up toward it, that she chooses to force open. She is still thinking about the driver, about the baby daughter he will continue to share, even with those more ordinary. And she thinks about breaking a glass once she is finished drinking from it.

But the waiter does not bring her anything to drink; the waiter does not bring her any glass to break. In fact, he does not see her sitting at a table with three empty chairs around her. The room with its blue light and burning candles holds her like the quiet centre of a flame. With her hands folded on the red table she waits, smiling at the couples and old men, nodding at a woman wearing black corduroy who rubs against everyone like a large, sad cat to the washroom and back, to the washroom and back.

Yes, the corduroy cat-woman seemed to be the only one to acknowledge the ordinary woman sitting alone with three chairs. Her waiting lasted four minutes, though she felt it like it were forty-four. The waiter saw her only when she rose to leave. And the cat-woman, coming out of the washroom. She saw her push the door open and slip through without letting in any snow or wind to upset the candles. Slip away because there was nothing else she could properly do.

The Molested in the Mirror

Noni, Who Needed To Cry

We loved Noni: his short dark hair and thin moustache, his muscular arms, his freckled hands. We loved him and hated to see him moping about, dragging his feet in the sand. We read books that said we needed to help, that Noni's sadness might never go away. So, what happened to Noni? His sister died in a fire, his girlfriend left him for Spain, he failed and failed all his written tests, every oral exam. Noni wandered in and out of our houses; Noni wrestled with his father on the small brown lawn. Noni's mother said they might send Noni and his new attitude away. So we took him to the river and sat him there and said he had to cry. Said he had to find that desperate dog inside himself and drown him down in tears. Noni, our good friend, complied. He sat on a stone and started to weep. After three hours we said Noni, you can stop now, you've drowned him — we see that sad dog floating! But Noni could not stop. He cried and cried for days. He cries there today.

The Molested in the Mirror

The molested in the mirror makes no sense to himself
and he's going to be a wolf for Halloween

The sheep behind him is a sneaky sheep
but this sheep will not be able to steady himself

Come first snowfall, come Christmastime

Intersection with Strawberries

Slipped loose from hospital, strangers might think strawberries afloat in black, puddle, rain. Crushed long streetcar, down by sewer. Seventeen red Horns blast against her bones: blue hands spilling, housedress slipping. Escaped from hospital, strangers might think when they see strawberries down sewer and suck down summer.

I fell, slipping strangers.

I dropped strawberries down summer. Years ago I might have made it across not breaking with the fallen birds, black puddles of rain, wet newspapers on the road. But the young are afraid to help me; they think when will you rise to strike me? Old Lady, how can you stop me interfering with the last sweet dream of your life?

Cupboard

Some people have ideas that resemble things they keep locked in cabinets: jewels, for example, or crystal high up on shelves sparkling down on those of us who cannot reach. Our ideas resemble that which most comfortably surrounds us: books, maps, sky, wind, trees, concrete. My thoughts, kept in darkness, are like spices I rely on for cooking. Here: let me show you my turmeric, paprika, nutmeg.

Poem on the Stairs

I keep tripping over the poem
on the stairs

a beggar-doll
with tangled hair
and missing limbs

naked to the waist
and wearing

one blue shoe for walking
partway.

I have no daughter
so it must be me
who keeps leaving her
here, dishevelled

little thing, homeless
on the narrow
steps.

Urban Restaurant

My forks are Chinese ideograms; my knives
draw ink from the stiff linen cloth.

We've a snake to take care of the mice.
He suns himself in a crooked line on the patio stairs.

I'm in love with Ezra, the new saucier,
who speaks six languages

and leaves no fingerprints
on the large white plates.

Thirteen Ways of Looking at Jason Brown

I

Here is Jungle Jason
asleep in the acajou tree
his fingernails dirty
from digging

II

The two green eyes of the dump cat
belong to Jason Brown

III

I see Jason
the pomegranate
on Thursday

I see Jason
the artichoke
on Sunday

IV

At the diggity-dog party
they said Jason Brown
tastes like tamarind
and no one
disagreed

v

Jason still thinks about Medea
in her purple dress

vi

Where is Jason's wheelbarrow?
Where is his boat?

vii

Borges and the Red Monster. Trains.
White Narcissus, Pad Thai, Newsprint.

This is all we know about Jason Brown.

viii

lower-case jay
lives on the rim
of kate's teacup

where her mouth
moves
every morning

IX

JASON BROWN GIVES GREEN SWEATER AWAY

X

Dear Jason:

I dreamed you grew a long beard; I dreamed
you were poisoned by green grapes. I hope
you are good and safe.

XI

It's Jason waiting outside
the Grace Church, but no
top hat? No bow tie?

XII

Jason is asleep beside her awake on the airplane over the
ocean

XIII

Jason, let me see you smile
on the footbridge

Song for a Salty Man Made of Stones

I'm full of limping metres, halting rhymes,
just a jingle can I make my way
to him who married her, trick this skirt
into a jaunty lilt

To make things better, make him want to
take her into and keep the rhyme on
like a tight black dress, here, where it zips straight
up — *ouch* his love

Drifts away and circles back again — it's a kite,
but I'm not holding on anymore
to black butterflies, old letters, yellow pictures
of them I loved so deeply

When I smell him in all the air, salty man
made of stones buried in cold water

O young husband, O black dog,
O green rainstorm, O tall fire
in the fireplace.

In bed I pray one thousand prayers for you
that want to go from me, for you that may return

Can Be Kind

They can be Kind, but most often it is not a matter of Kindness. Most often they simply want what they want and Kindness works. Kindness works wonders, works under water, works even when you feel under the weather. When I'm lonely I think about things like this: Kindnesses and Wants and Ways. The cracks in walls and perfect round plates. The Kindness of dogs and stones and innocent mistakes. I am prone to fits of rhyming. I try to keep the jingle in check. I use Kindness to help me. I am a Kindness scientist. I own tools: scalpels, spoons, scissors. Bulbous and slender bottles, numerous sharp rulers. With these objects I measure Kindness; I dissect Kindness. I specialize in Kindnesses that have contracted Cancer. It is strange, and it saddens me to have to keep certain kinds of Kindnesses in cages. But the cage is in case of escape. The cage is in case of cruelty. Retaliation, infection. I sleep with my patients. I know it is perverse, but some late nights after so much cutting and scraping, I find myself caressing that which I have dug from the tender body of the anaesthetized Kindness. I find I have taken the hard-wild bit of blood and bone into my mouth. I find myself climbing into the cage.

I believe in reward, in a cure. I trust in the potential for Kindness Healthiness. I intend to promote the implementation of Universal Kindness Study, despite the weaknesses of my own scientific abilities.

Lullaby for Martin

I want to go to Ždala, my lonely village
I want to go to Ždala, my cold hands

Martin my brother, Martin my twin
You left me behind

Little one, don't play with matches in the cornfield
Little one, don't burn your eyes so you can't see me

The wind makes your shirt dance like a flag
The wind catches fire in your hands

Little one of roses, our mother is sleeping
Little one of fire, father will come find you

You turned into a small tree
You burned down to thin black branches

I want to go to Ždala, my lonely village
I want to go to Ždala, my cold hands

Martin my brother, Martin my twin
I left you behind

Happiness

You are my little wolf, my naked man
in the morning. You find my sad ankles
like spurs that jingle jangle jingle.

You are my tuxedo, my rose.

The Fitting Room

No one will tell you why you do not love
your body anymore, why they are laughing *hee haw hee*
in the lingerie shops, one tall woman for every small dark room.
Here you will meet your fat
and shadow, enter
into your nakedness formally, with a
sense of art and ceremony.

Beloved, be alone
and beware of Greta, do not buy
the antique dress. Repeat this
to soothe yourself while making your way through:
nothing fits nothing fits nothing fits.

Look to the fitting room of the future: leather
couches, better lighting, locks
that make a click sound you can be sure of.

Remember there is something in each private compartment
that aspires to greatness; once I heard a lady weep
because she didn't want to come out.

Toronto, City of Sad Faces

Careful Ophelia on the streetcar, kissing him.
Your mother can't keep her mask on straight.

Outside the liquor store: I love you. I don't
love you. I love you I don't love. Moving Day.

She sleeps on perfumed cement. Her cold ear
waits for music, his hard clown shoes in the street.

Elevator mirrors, shopping bags, dishevelled pigeons.
Malachite, obsidian for sale. Come closer.

He hums inside his solitary body, flourishes
on the subway, unfolds stiff newspaper wings.

Ships, slugs on the horizon.
The sun slips down in you.

Daughter, let the raccoon in.
Hold his cold hand.

Skin Poem

In time the skin
makes perfect sense: we talk
in bed

arms and legs
tongue-tied

until the words come.

Elegy for Atlas

You were a mutt, like us kids, all mixed up inside.

I watched you.
The summer you chewed off your tail
to forestall the divorce.

The spring you dug a small hole
under the fence and forced yourself
out.

It was raining. You looked so sad
when we found you, your wet black nose
muddy and profound.

We dragged you back, but none of us knew
where home was anymore.

When we were children we gave you potato chips.
We folded your heart pills into salty slices of cheese.

And when it was time to grow up and move out
you pissed on all the boxes, barked

a whole dog song
into an empty bowl.

Trains

Sometimes she lets the baby cry
to watch her oldest boy

with his small hands winding wooden trains
over the bridge, up by the wrecking yard,

down past the lake and pine trees.

Through his imaginary countryside
they travel on two tracks, careless Mommy

takes charge of the passenger cars
while he handles the freight.

She fears her derailment would make him happy,
concedes to a collision.

No one dies, he reassures her, just a few
get hurt.

First Husband

Like the young girl in that book
I murdered him in the afternoon.

His policies were killing me so I
poured a little varnish in his wine.

We kissed and I waited. Now he was heavy
and I was light! I was light.

I had longed to drag him, let
his head bump and knock on the antiques.

His hair got a little mucky, but no matter.
I lifted him into the canoe. Sat him up.

I opened his eyes and cleaned the mud off his neck.
Shortly after, I shoved him off.

I kept rowing in the lake, came to Hamilton, remarried.
Look now, at my garden. Look at this lovely tree

with the swing on it.

The Foyer of Formal Feeling

Riding Hood Reads the Suicide Note

Your Nana loved the wolf. My dear, I was afraid
what you might think. Remember I am buried
in his skin; it was what I wanted all along: a muzzle
of blood and fur, a long nocturnal life. You must learn
to love those who trespass; they are the most interesting
people you will come across.

Feelings go first of all to the fire. Save the ears
for second last and the wolf's eyes will go down easy.

The Conversationalist

O, the little white mice in her imaginary laboratory! Nina could not get enough of torturing them, sometimes taking their pink feet into her mouth. Truth be told: Nina was a failure. Nina was stupidly silent. All she had were the mice. White mice with pink feet and hot, red eyes that looked up at her with a kind of evil love.

Words, Nina thought, and sentences that fit together exactly the way Anna's do, Anna, her cousin, the Conversationalist. Anna, who made her opinions known. Not like Nina with nothing but little white mice in her head!

Poor Nina!

The Foyer of Formal Feeling

Emily D. is quiet. She hesitates in the hall
where her grey hats and feelings are.

Her shoes are small in his hands. Closeted: two moths
feast on a coat that will not cry out.

Silence is akin to pain. Do you think so, Emily D.?
Her forehead wrinkles; he reads the poem there.

Love for Jennifer

She is alone in her bedroom, watching a small television. Three of her friends have recently married. Jennifer is heavy, her eyes deep-set and blue. The bombing will continue through Ramadan and Christmastime and she will do nothing to stop it. She has a faraway feeling, even her dreams feel peripheral, and this war is like that. No different. It simply hasn't come. Love for Jennifer like a perfumed letter lost in the mail. She waits up with the late-night news, searches the crowd, reads his lips.

Love for Jennifer. Love for Jennifer.
Believe in me. I am here.

Rain and Lemon Cookies

I close Rain out now
Yes — making love, rain reminds me

Young skin we used to live in, puddles on our wedding day
the tallest, gravest husband dancing

Time is mine alone to rouge up
these wrinkled cheeks   cut clean   sweep

Little bits of him (hair, toenails, eyelashes) alongside dead parts
growing long after he's gone

Do I Rain? Do I Shame on loving
like a little girl? The final days are hard lemon cookies

cut in flat flower shapes, broken on my tongue

The Refrigerator Memory

The mustard is hard yellow hot mustard, Keen's in a small glass jar. I remember when you chose it against all other mustards; no matter what happens I will never throw it away. The chicken is wrapped carefully but looks cold and angry. One, two, three little olives floating in the brine of my brain. The beets were beside you; the beets said *we think badly of you and the way you behaved at the funeral.* I cut my hands on the fish in the freezer. The solid mass of corn I take to the sink is the size of your head: I try to crack it apart. The radishes are black and wet but I wash them and salt them until they stand no more of my tears. I toast the stale butt end of the bread. I hate it when my tongue touches down on the strawberry jam.

I stopped eating because it was too painful. My sister suggested I try ingesting different things. Different from what I ate with you. Like what? Like anchovies and rice, she said. Like smelts on black bread. Like fruit punch. Like beef tongue and blood pudding. Things she likes. New things. Don't eat anything you know he hated; don't eat anything you know he loved. He's gone. And you're not going to starve yourself on my watch. Get up. Get ready. We're going to that new Ethiopian restaurant downtown. I've already made the reservation.

New Ethiopian restaurant?

We used to make a game of finishing all the supplies we had in our apartment before we would go out into the real world to buy more. We'd boil the last egg, slice the final pickle, jam the limp celery down into the blender to make cold soup. And when the late-night news came on in our bedroom we felt ashamed for being so gluttonous. We drank our wine until we passed out and forgot about them, the poorest people on earth, people who could not make a game of their nothingness, people who would not have found our empty freezer very funny.

＊

You're fixated! This *fridge* is for *food.* But I had hidden the mustard. The swollen garbage bag leaked a brown tear across the kitchen floor.

Little Pica

The child tastes it: sadness in the blood. Feeds
on her first companion.

Chalk and clay, coal and matches singe the calendar squares away.

She takes the dead flame to her mother's mouth, acquires
her own taste for red elements: dust, fire, broken stones
kicked up the cold path.

She sucks pennies, keys, nails me down
in her dream of perfect bones for new fresh hands.

House for Sale by Owner

Clumps of wet towel console the broken
toilet, here's a solitary sunken candle

in the handsome claw tub. This old
rug burned away in the bedroom; one

yellow curtain still stinks of fire.
Shame on you, my hanging lady! (the sloppy

fence, she breaks down) when we go
to the yard.

*

The yard, the yard: two rusting
bicycles bend toward each other

and it's like coming across teenage
bones, young love. At night

I have ghosts rattling in the knife
drawer, uneven ghosts I most regret.

I leave them, damn devils.
They are musical.

They have no place to go.

Dirty Rapunzel

Paradise! No fly to find the corner of the mouth, no candy wrapper stuck to the sole of your shoe. Hills and stone houses with flat solid faces, small trees on tiny lawns and the larger ones plump and jolly in parks where they should be. This is a city, after all, the tall buildings remain white and fantastic, the summer hot with humans drooping and dreaming in windows. This is the future and there are no screens, no porches. I am alone like everyone else, leaning out, my long brown hair fallen against the wall like a dirty Rapunzel.

Someone is stepping on my toes, but who is it? Is it Nancy, slamming her car door, bringing up a bottle of red wine in the afternoon? Nancy sitting and talking about architecture and her autistic son and her husband who is charming but seems to be putting on a bit of weight? Nancy talks for hours. I interrupt. I interrupt by introducing the subject of fish and the future and it all goes to hell. *Not the damn fish again!* she says. I start to cough and Nancy pours herself another glass of California wine.

She returns every week. She is relieved to find me alive and well, open and anticipatory. (My pelvic bone a sand-stone sculpture heavy on the ledge. The latent sun and slant-ed shadow on my face.) Nancy has her reasons. A distant memory, she once said quietly. I am going to take you far away. No more love like porches and screens and flies in the corner of the mouth.

And this is how it will happen: A little boy wearing a blue hat will cry out *Rapunzel, Rapunzel, let down your hair!*

They will say I lost my balance suntanning my arms. They will note my habit of listening for laughter in the street.

They will be kind to my sister.

Brussels Sprout

I want one
someday, a Baby, little

brussels sprout to salt
and butter

and love. To become
a mother and savour

the small green life
so round and rolling

on the flat
dinner plate, thinking
dreaming

thinking. To know my
Baby like the bitter

centre of the world.

The Runaway Budgie

Honey do you remember the green bird we found dead under the porch, the runaway budgie? Yes, we took that bony bird with his bent green feathers and gave him a proper burial. You touched him with your bare hands and I was amazed. He was already full of worms.

Sweetie everyone says that I've got a 'real zest for life' but I'm just dishonest. I've got white hair now and I'm always fantasizing about my death. What a laugh I am, smiling over my lukewarm soup!

Darling the doctor wants to operate, before it gets too cold, thinks it would be nice for me to recuperate in September when the leaves start to change.

Honey I guess I'll just keep doing what I've been doing.

Sweetie Hell. Darling Hell. Honey Hell.

Oh Sweetie! Yesterday I found two small shells in your coat pocket. My Love I felt ridiculous for being alive to find them.

Sunburn

Sometimes the sunshine on top will not stop. Yesterday shows up everywhere and hurts to be touched. They might not even notice the little ember

in your bedroom and say that 'something of the sunburn sated her; after all the temperature of her skin kept rising like a premonition.'

Snakes and Bees

1 Memo

Attention, snakes and bees: the trapeze artist has retired.
Please note that all of the parrot's fine plumage has been
donated to the octopus.

Somewhere bread is burning, you are humming, the edges of
lost letters are turning yellow.

2 Poem

My telephone is trying
to swallow herself again, rotating her tired axis, clicking.

A washed bone, she's become the last of you, your left leg.
Look at the way I cradle it.

The Hot-Air Balloon Operator and Her Brother

The day Wilomena Jeanette Parker renounced her years of
university study to become a Hot-Air Balloon Operator
was a sad day for the entire Parker family. Wilomena's
brother, Clement Parker, took it the hardest. He took it to
heart, in fact, and would not speak to his sister for sixteen
days. On the seventeenth, Wilomena's birthday, he decided
to forgive her and went out by himself to the field where
she worked.

Wilomena, who might have been a medical doctor, was
wearing all white. Her long brown hair drifted up among
ropes that fastened the balloon to its basket. Clement Parker
stood beside his car with a piece of chocolate cake for her
on a stiff paper plate. The late afternoon sky was cloudless,
endless. The balloon was purple, regal, not ridiculous the
way he had imagined it would be. His sister stood with a
grey-haired man who held a small black terrier in his arms.
Dear Wilomena, he thought, I hope you know what you are
doing.

Clement made his way across the field looking down at
the grass, at his patent-leather shoes sinking in the mud.
Wilomena, already in the basket with the elderly man and
his dog, called out to her brother to hurry if he wanted to
come for a ride. Clement was surprised by his sudden desire
to go up with his sister, by his fear of being left behind. He
steadied the chocolate cake with his thumb and ran toward
her in a way he hadn't done in many years.

Once in the balloon, Clement found himself silenced
by the barking dog. The pointed tops of pine trees, the

black-roofed houses, the narrow backyards and disappearing rock gardens all filled him with a terrible sorrow.

Wilomena stood close to the old man, letting the terrier lick the chocolate icing off her fingers, laughing. This was the moment Clement thought he might strangle her, the moment he imagined his sister's body dropping down through the sky, landing broken near the front steps, back home where he might help her start again.

Pelican

If your eyes are cornflower blue and I describe them (that way) how does it make you feel? Also, your skin resembles the wet, white inside of a cut green apple and that is why I am always here and biting down. You have crumbs in the corners of your eyes, a moody disposition, sometimes you remind me of a pelican. You horde fish and you want everyone to remember you. I play with your cat. Pretend to feel. Possessive. When, you, bend, to, kiss, me, you taste like Pelee Island honey. I often wonder what we would look like in the forest, your thin belly full of maple syrup, my hair sticky?

Snowstorm

Proximity: eager, available, lovely. Goddess of the human
body snowstorm winterbird. The Ghost of Christmas Past

hangs the witch of this winter, toppling snowmen
collecting the coal eyes of each found lover. Clumsy

Faith Magic no match for her, Proximity
knows she is nearest

owns the space. Words die

The Father-Daughter Dance

in memory of Yehuda Amichai

Yehuda is mine. Tears
piggyback words like a small girl
carried uphill by her father.

In Yemen, Moshe
Yehuda is dying. Leaving me
the way they all do, with
the same excuse:

I thought it was love
but it was cancer

Cancer the benign flower
I pinned to your lapel. Cancer
the lily corsage, withered
on my wrist.

Yehuda, be honest.
If I come to Jerusalem,
will you still take me
to the father-daughter
dance?

Triptych

for my mother

✦

Mary is on the roof again.
Here is her hammer; here is her carpenter-husband
cutting wood in cold shade.

✦

I'M ALL THE NAILS IN THIS SMALL BOX
she shouts, shaking them at the sky.

✦

dear god
i'm a tiny window
with a perfect
blue pane

Notes

1 Ždala is a tiny village located on the Northern border of Croatia; 'Lullaby for Martin' (page 48) is a translation of an imaginary Croatian lullaby. Martin (Miter) was my grandmother's twin brother, just a little boy when he died after accidentally setting himself on fire while playing with matches in a corn field. Although there are no living relatives left in Ždala, the remaining villagers still tend Martin's grave.

2 'The Foyer of Formal Feeling' (page 61) was inspired by Emily Dickinson's beautiful little poem #341, which begins:

> After great pain, a formal feeling comes—
> The Nerves sit ceremonious, like tombs—

3 Some pregnant women develop a rare condition called pica, which is a compulsion to eat substances such as chalk, coal, toothpaste, burnt matches, dirt and clay. 'Little Pica' (page 66) refers to this condition. Although many theories have been put forward to explain this strange habit, none have been widely accepted.

Acknowledgements

Early versions of some of these poems and miniatures have appeared in *Grain, Queen Street Quarterly, OFF THE SHELF, Exile: The Literary Quarterly, THIS, Gaspereau Review, Zarez, PRISM international* and in the chapbook *poem(s) on the stairs*, published by above/ground press.

Thanks to my family and friends, especially my sweet husband David Derry, for caring about poetry and for being the first to lay eyes on many of these poems.

Jet and John, for their love and help with Sadie Glenn.

Steve Bacic, for attending readings rain or shine.

Thanks, also, to the Banff Centre for the Arts and Wired Writing Studio, the Ontario Media Development Corporation, the Eastend Arts Council (Saskatchewan), the Canada Council for the Arts, the Toronto Arts Council and the Ontario Arts Council, for supporting this project at various stages of its development.

Special thanks to Coach House Books and Alana Wilcox for excellent editorial advice, support and new friendship.

Finally, I would like to thank Annabel Lyon and her new baby, and Patrick Friesen for being Patrick Friesen.

Typeset in Centaur and printed and bound at
the Coach House on bpNichol Lane, 2005.

Edited and designed by Alana Wilcox
Cover painting by Brad Harley
Cover design by Rick/Simon

Coach House Books
401 Huron Street (rear) on bpNichol Lane
Toronto, Ontario M5S 2G5

416 979 2217
800 367 6360

www.chbooks.com
mail@chbooks.com